A GIFT FOR:

FROM:

Published by Hallmark Gift Books,
a division of Hallmark Cards, Inc.,
Kansas City, MO 64141
Visit us on the Web at Hallmark.com.

Editorial Director: Delia Berrigan
Editor: Kim Schworm Acosta
Art Director: Chris Opheim
Designer: Brian Pilachowski
Production Designer: Dan Horton

ISBN: 978-1-59530-800-9
BOK9233

Made in China
AUG15

LIFE REFLECTIONS

SHORE
LINES

FROM THE BEACH

Hallmark

CLOUDS
-MAY-
HIDE THE SUN
BUT ONLY FOR
A LITTLE WHILE.

EVERY DAY

& EVERY TIDE

bring new treasures to your shores.

Being *true* to *yourself* comes with scary moments.

But it's so very worth it.

Make time to
PLAY.

EVEN THE SUN NEEDS DOWNTIME.

THE STRONG MAY SWIM,
THE FEARFUL MAY FLOUNDER,
THE LAZY MAY DRIFT,

BUT THE OCEAN CARRIES THEM ALL.

COLLECT SMALL JOYS.

*Wherever you go,
leave a trail of*
HAPPY

MEMORIES.

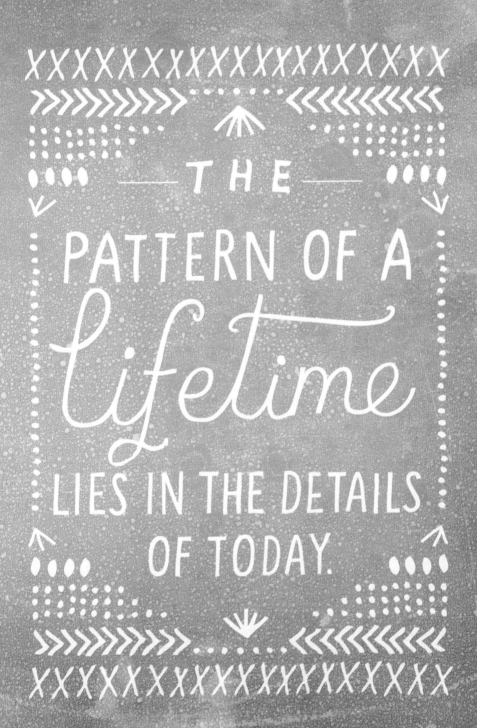

Rest
upon the cool grass.

Linger
in the golden sun.

Dream
beneath the
bright blue sky.

THE TIDE

ALWAYS TURNS.

Each of us carries a

SUNRISE

within.

THERE IS MEANING
IN SILENCE
AS WELL AS
IN WORDS.

SEEK WHA,
THE SOUL

CRAVES.

Sometimes it helps just to know

YOU'RE NOT ALONE.

Nobody else's
FOO

TEPS

*lead exactly
where you're going.*

TELL YOUR STORY & BE THE LIGHT THAT HELPS OTHERS FIND THEIR WAY.

LOOK AROUND.
LIFE COMES with

GREAT VIEW.

We marvel at the POWER
Yet, within each

f the sea.

f us is a FORCE

that's mightier.

Life is like a day at the beach—

if you're not careful,
YOU'LL GET BURNED.
If you're too careful,
YOU WON'T HAVE ANY FUN.

We will be known

FOREVER B

THE RIPPLES
we create.

BE STILL
& LET YOUR
HEART dream.

For every
—JOY—
that passes,
something
❧ BEAUTIFUL ❧
remains.

Find your INNER beach.

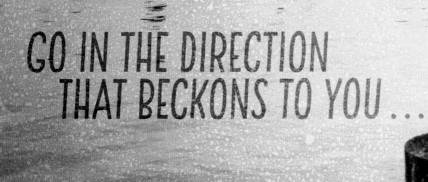

GO IN THE DIRECTION
THAT BECKONS TO YOU ...

AND IT WILL LEAD TO *your* GREATEST ADVENTURES.

WAVES

MAKE

WAVES

MAKE

WAVES.

LET *life* TAKE YOU SOMEWHERE *magical.*

DO your THING.

A NEW
DREAM
IS ALWAYS, ALWAYS
SHIMMERING
ON THE
HORIZON.

THE OCEAN
doesn't worry

when the

TIDE IS LOW.

Gather as many
dreams
as you like.

No one needs to

choose just one.

Toss worries to the *breeze.*

BEAUTY
AROUND US,

BEAUTY

WITHIN US.

Like the smell of SALT
in your hair,
like warm SAND
between your toes,
let HAPPINESS stay
with you all day long.

If you have enjoyed this book
or it has touched your life in some way,
we would love to hear from you.

Please send your comments to:
Hallmark Book Feedback
P.O. Box 419034
Mail Drop 100
Kansas City, MO 64141

Or e-mail us at:
booknotes@hallmark.com